THE GOLDEN BOOK OF SPONSORSHIP

By
Father John Doe
(Rev. Ralph Pfau)
Author
of
SOBRIETY AND BEYOND
SOBRIETY WITHOUT END

* * *

Hazelden Publishing
Center City, Minnesota 55012-0176
hazelden.org/bookstore

© 1953 by Hazelden Foundation.
First published 1953
by SMT Guild, Inc., Indianapolis.
First published by Hazelden 1998

All rights reserved
Printed in the United States of America
No portion of this publication may be reproduced in any manner
without the written permission of the publisher

ISBN: 978-1-56838-236-4

In Memoriam

Doherty Sheerin

founder of A.A. in Indiana, and the author's sponsor

Died January 27, 1953, having enjoyed,
with the help of God and A.A.,
fifteen years of continuous sobriety.
May God grant him eternal peace and
serenity—of which Dohr gave so much to so many.

"This Is a *Give* Program"

*"What we give away—we keep; for it is in
    the giving that we receive:
What we keep to ourselves we lose; for in the
    keeping we cannot reproduce:
And when we die, we take with us only that which
    we have given away."*

Gratitude

"Were not ten made clean? Where are the other nine?"

We're a nation of pet owners, and while cat-lovers are legion, dogs seem to have even more universal appeal. The reason most people like dogs is that dogs are such *grateful* animals. You rub them behind the ears, and they grovel with gratitude at your feet. You bring them their food, and they run to you, barking their appreciation and frisking about you with a friendliness that warms even the most forlorn heart. However hungry the dog may be, he takes time out to first look up at you with a misty thank-you in his eyes, which is unmistakable even before he begins to gulp his food down. When, on a cold winter day, you let him come into the house, he repays you his thanks by his tail wagging which seems endless. And when you are gone for a while and return home even after a brief absence, he welcomes you with an enthusiasm that makes your return seem to have been a very special favor to him.

But cats on the average are very selfish creatures. Even when they appear to rub themselves affectionately and gratefully against your leg, you seem to sense that they are doing it for purely sensory satisfaction. They purr and they press against you, not because you happen to be you and they are grateful, but because they delight in their fur being rubbed back into place and in the pleasure they receive from it. Feed them, and they take their food with a sniffy-like condescension. Allow them a place near the heater, and they bask in its warmth, close their eyes, and proceed to drift into self-satisfied slumber without so much as a glance, grateful or contemptuous, in your direction.

Dogs are extroverts, pouring themselves out upon you. They are continually conscious of what is and what moves about them.

Cats are introverts, living in a smug little world of their own and always seeking therein their own comfort and convenience. It is only some happening that might provoke a fear of being disturbed that will awaken them to the surrounding events.

Dogs are loyal and show a loyal gratitude to a master irrespective of the type of master he or she may be. It is because of this that a dog will follow his master, even though such master might be indifferent or even cruel, and he will follow that master into poverty, walk at his heels over the most uncomfortable roads, leave a cozy home for a miserable cabin, and then act all the while as if he were privileged to be accompanying his master.

Many a cat, on the other hand, will watch the best of masters go away and calmly and unperturbedly remain behind in the comfortable house, which it much prefers to any human companionship. Even after a stray cat has been warmed and fed and housed for the night, try to coax it outside with you the next day if the weather be foul, and you will find that the recipient of all of your favors will choose not to show its gratitude by following you, but selfishly remain inside the shelter of your abode. Indeed, if you want a cat to go with you, the only way usually is to force it along in your carrier. From the viewpoint of the average cat, you personally happen to be just a convenience to which it has grown accustomed and which, if necessary, it can easily do without.

To a dog you are his world—you are his everything. And his tail is continually wagging in sonnets of gratitude. His bark, and even his playful growl—yes, even his snapping—is usually a song of thanksgiving. And when he cavorts before you, he flings himself about with gestures of worship that no pagan ever accorded to his idol. He loves you for the scraps from the table no matter how meager, and he is likewise appreciative for even an idle stroking of his head which you at times may do in absent-mindedness. And above all, he never fails to let you know it!

And that is probably why we like dogs. We all love gratitude and always react with a warm glow to the act of appreciation, to the note of thanks, to the letter of gratitude. And maybe that is the real reason some people don't like cats—their ingratitude shows, and we dislike the ingrate. And yet, there are very, very many humans in this old world who are ungrateful or at least who never take the time to show their gratitude. We hesitate to label such as ingrates—perhaps a better term would be "thoughtless" in place of "thankless." But the fact remains: most people are not grateful in *action,* no matter how deep the *feeling* of appreciation may penetrate on the occasion of a favor or kindness or gift. And it is without doubt because of this that the act of kindness whatsoever it may have been dies within the heart to which it was given—for it was not returned to its donor nor was it in appreciation passed on to another. "What we keep to ourselves we lose; for in the keeping we cannot reproduce" for self-containment is but synonymous with sterility.

For the past six years the writer has been enabled to publish the Golden Book Series—one each successive year. The thoughts in these booklets are first gathered together a year before publication. They are then used as the theme of our Alcoholics Anonymous Retreats for that year. The following spring the thoughts are put in writing, and another one of the Golden Books becomes a reality. On publication, we have always sent to our very personal friends a copy of the new booklet with our compliments. On the average about a hundred are thus mailed out. But you know something? Of this hundred, only about eight or ten are acknowledged, and those only over a period of the ensuing year.

Then came 1952. *The Book of Excuses* had been published and copies had been dispatched to friends here and there. The A.A. Retreat time was fast approaching. Our mental faculties seemed to become more and more sterile as the time approached. A new theme for the coming year seemed not to be found. Then we received a letter. It read as follows:

Dear _____,

I hope this reaches you. For want of a return address I am sending this to the publishing company. I do want you to know how much I've appreciated every one of your books. They never fail to galvanize and inspire me, and I keep going back to them again and again.

If your books can mean this much to someone without an alcoholic problem, I can imagine what a lifeline they are to alcoholics. God love them all!

Please remember me in your prayers. And thank you again for sharing your inspiration and wonderful work with me.

Sincerely,

The writer's signature appeared below the closing.

We immediately thought of something that had happened many, many years ago and had to do with ten men who had leprosy. The story goes like this:

> And as He entered a certain village, there met Him ten men who were lepers. They stood afar off and lifted up their voices and said, "Jesus, Master, have mercy on us." And when He saw them he said to them, "Go show yourselves to the priests." And it came to pass that as they went they were cleansed.
>
> And one of them, when he saw that he was healed, turned back and with a loud voice glorified God. And fell down on his face at His feet, giving Him thanks: and he was a Samaritan.
>
> And Jesus answering said, "Were not ten made clean? Where are the other nine? There are none found to return and give glory to God, save this stranger.

And then another thought came to mind. We thought of the question that is being asked all over the country in A.A., "Where are the old-timers in A.A.? So many no longer take an interest in the group. So few will sponsor new members. Many no longer attend meetings. Where are they?"

And then we mused to ourselves: "Were not all of them made sober? Where are the other nine?"

We forgot to tell you that the letter quoted above was from a nonalcoholic. But its contents should have told you that. And what was it Christ said? "There are none found to return...save this *stranger*." And he was a Samaritan.

And the letter writer was a *nonalcoholic*.

And now all these ideas coalesced: "The other nine" human ingratitude; human thoughtlessness; failure to recognize a gift; A.A. leakage; the Twelfth Step: "Having had a spiritual awakening...we tried to carry..."; we received; we give.

At last we had our theme: *Gratitude,* the Twelfth Step in *action*.

Gratitude and A.A.

*"So that you, being strengthened,
may in turn strengthen your fellow man..."*

No one ever really got "on the program" of A.A. without taking the First Step. Likewise, no one ever stayed on the program without continuing to the Twelfth Step. For in the Twelfth Step is all the activity that insures, enlarges upon, and matures our sobriety and our serenity. "Having had a spiritual awakening we (in turn) tried to carry the message to alcoholics." In this we have expressed again in a little different way the so-called paradox of living: "We keep only what we give away; for it is in the giving that we receive." In the Twelfth Step also we have indicated to us the value of gratitude in action. In it we have enunciated to us the principle that "all gifts are given to us by Almighty God in order that we may give them in turn to our fellowman." And that is true gratitude.

This whole idea was explained to Peter when he was made head of the apostles. He was told at that time "I have prayed for you, Peter, that your faith fail you not... so that *you, being strengthened, may in turn strengthen your fellow man.*" This is merely another way of telling him, and us, that all of God's gifts are loaned to us, and that we keep them only as we in our gratitude in turn share them with our fellow man. And so, too, our sobriety in A.A. is loaned to us, so that we in turn *may give it to other alcoholics.* And the funny thing is, bub, that is *the only way* we can keep it! And the heartbreaking experiences of many, many "slippees" bear tragic testimony to this truth.

But someone about this time is going to object. And they are going to say, "If it is gratitude that makes the Twelfth Step work, then how about the fact that we are always being told this is a "selfish" program? And such a one will insist: "Gratitude comes from love, and what has love to do with selfishness?"

We shall endeavor to answer. And first of all may we point out what many seem to overlook, namely that the "selfish" part we so often are told about means we must take care of self *first*. For we are reminded again and again in A.A. that if we don't stay sober ourselves we won't be of any use to anyone or anybody. And so A.A. is definitely a "selfish" program, for it teaches *prudent self-love*. But so does the law of love! What is it that we are taught? "Thou shalt love the Lord thy God with thy whole heart. . . and thy neighbor as thyself." Which means we must love our self first—prudent selfishness!

Thus in the Twelfth Step we learn that we shall keep our sobriety only if we in turn give it to someone else. And therefore, in order to keep it, in order to preserve ourselves, we carry the message to other alcoholics, which means we practice and continue to practice the Twelfth Step in order to keep sober ourselves. And that gives us the *motive* for doing it: a motive that cannot puff us up, a motive that will keep us humble, a motive that will not make us become patronizing, a motive that will continue to remind us of our need, a motive, finally, that will enable the pathologically proud alcoholic to practice love of his fellowman and to show gratitude to his fellow man and still avoid getting on the pedestal of the philanthropist.

The founder of our A.A. group in Indianapolis had a pet phrase. Seldom did he give a talk in A.A. without repeating it again and again. It was a simple phrase. In a very few words it expressed the whole gist of success in A.A., particularly in practicing the Twelfth Step. The phrase he so often used is, "This is a *give* program."

Again we hear the echo. "It is in giving that we receive." "We keep only what we give away." "So that you being strengthened, you may in turn strengthen your fellow man."

Yes, chum, this is a selfish program; but it is not a *take* program; it is a *give* program.

The Twelfth Step

"Having had a spiritual awakening as the result of these steps, we tried to carry this message to alcoholics and to practice these principles in all of our affairs."

In the Twelfth Step we have three definite actions. One passive, one active, and one both active and passive.

1. "Having *had* a spiritual awakening;" herein we are passive; we receive; the "compulsion to drink is expelled by Almighty God." As it is phrased in many A.A. circles: "The expulsion of a compulsion by a Higher Power." God has *given* us sobriety along with an entire new spiritual attitude.

2. "We tried to *carry the message* to alcoholics;" and herein we begin to *give;* we become *active;* we share with others what has been given to us.

3. "And *practice* these principles in all of *our affairs*;" and herein we *continue* to be *active* on *ourselves*—"in all of our affairs;" we *act* on *ourselves* and then are *passive* in *accepting* its discipline. As the Big Book of *Alcoholics Anonymous* tells us, we are "disciplining ourselves into habits of unselfishness and love."

One of the first mistakes made by many in A.A. relative to the Twelfth Step is a misunderstanding of what the term "spiritual awakening" means.

There are two things that it is definitely *not:* it is not a *sudden* happening (except in very rare cases), and it is not *emotional*.

Perhaps if we analyzed the word "awakening" we may more easily understand it. All of us "awaken" every day from sleep. And what happens when we awaken? When we awaken, we usually *gradually* change from a state of sleep to a state of wakefulness. Seldom is it sudden. That is why we so often say we were only "half awake." For some it may take hours to have full use of one's faculties clearly after being in a deep sleep.

A similar circumstance takes place in A.A. We *gradually* awaken to a new life; a new attitude toward spiritual values; a new ability to think clearly. That is the spiritual awakening. So now we see things clearly. For the light of God's grace has entered our minds and our souls and has awakened our spirit to a new consciousness of Him. It is like all the things that we can see now, and hear now, and recognize now in the light of the new day, but which in the night and in slumber were totally invisible.

Whence does this "spiritual awakening" come? The Step is very explicit: "as a *result of these steps,*" that is, Steps One through Eleven. So therefore the Twelfth Step *presumes* that the other eleven have been taken.

If one is not conscious of having had a spiritual awakening, perhaps such a one might check: where are the other eleven?!

Having received this gift from God, we then begin to give. "We tried to carry this message to other alcoholics." And right here our little theory about motivation mentioned above will play a very, very important role.

If we carry the message, if we do Twelfth Step work, if we sponsor a new member in order to sober him or her up, we are likely to get into serious difficulty. For the prospect we are sponsoring *may* stay drunk. In fact, the first ten we sponsor may *all* stay drunk. And then what's going to happen with our motive? We are going to get an awfully bad case of self-pity. Poor guy! We tried and tried so hard—with *ten* of them—and they *all* stayed drunk. We simply must not be much good ourselves. And then—maybe a little drink might soothe our aching heart?!

Or it is possible that the first prospect we work on will stay sober and really "get" the program. It might even happen that the first *ten* we sponsor *might* stay sober and "get" the program. And then what is likely to happen? "Gosh, I must be some sponsor! Look, ten guys, and they are all on the program!" And then we go home and in our pride-fed elation we just might possibly look into the mirror. And we just might possibly admire that "big-shot" sponsor we see in the mirror. And then—we just might possibly invite that big-shot we are looking at out for a drink. It has happened!

On the other hand, if we sponsor a new member, if we carry the message in order to give away what we have *so that we may in turn keep it,* then it will not make any difference to us whether the new prospect stays sober or not because we have successfully accomplished what we set out to do. *We* have stayed sober. We have kept what we had because we gave it away irrespective of what the other fellow did with it.

What did we give away? What was the message? It is very simple: It is explained very tersely and very clearly in the Big Book: "Tell him what happened to you." In fact, that is all you have to give away—what happened to you—period.

"And practice these principles in all of our affairs." Which simply means putting into practice in all of our affairs, that is, in *all we do*—socially, spiritually, in business at home, in everything—all the things we learned and were given in the spiritual awakening. And "putting into practice" means repeating over and over—day in and day out; hour in and hour out; yet, if necessary, minute in and minute out.

"*So that you, being strengthened, may in turn strengthen your fellow man.*"

"Where are the other nine?" They stopped giving.

Carrying the Message

*"We tried to carry the message...
for it is in giving that we receive."*

When we "carry the message to other alcoholics," this giving of what was given to us is not confined to Twelfth-Step calls and sponsoring new members in A.A. Carrying the message includes *all* of what we refer to as "Twelfth-Step activity," including the living of the A.A. program.

So now let us review one by one all of those things sincere A.A.'s participate in as part of their Twelfth-Step living and all of which, too, they realize must be continued if they wish to retain sobriety, serenity, and happiness. We might say that the Twelfth Step is the "pay-off" step. For in pursuing it day in and day out, we keep on receiving a hundredfold in return in sobriety, in contentment, in peace of mind, in true friendships, in mutual esteem, and through it all and in it all we gradually grow and mature in body, mind, and soul.

1. **We give by attending meetings.** Many times we refer to A.A. meetings as a means of "insurance against a slip." The reason for this is that in giving by attending meetings, we receive and keep what was given to us—our sobriety, and an increase in serenity. But here again old man "motivation" comes in. Why do we go to meetings? Do we go to *give* or *get*? We will always get, and much, from meetings—*provided our purpose in going is to give,* if only by our presence to encourage the newcomers and others present. But if we primarily go to *get,* many, many times we shall leave the meeting empty-handed. For perhaps we went to hear a *good* talk and the speaker was "lousy." So all we take away is disappointment. Or perhaps we went to learn, and hearing nothing we did not already know, we again went away short of our expectations.

On the other hand, if we always go to the meetings to *give,* then no matter what might happen at the meetings, we shall always accomplish our purpose in going—an opportunity to *give* of ourselves. And then the One Who gave us our initial sobriety again gives the increase and the peace and the serenity. "For it is in the giving that we receive."

Furthermore, if we attend the meetings for what we receive from the talk, or associations with others, the time comes when these things are no longer attractive enough to motivate our attending. And so often then begin the excuses for staying away, for missing the meetings, because of the terrible speakers, or because they bore you to death, or because of this or that personality. But when we continue to attend meetings for *the purpose of giving in order to get and keep what we have,* we shall never be open to the deception of excuses for staying away. For no matter how bad the speaker may be, no matter how boring the meeting may be, no matter who is present or what takes place, *we still can and do accomplish our purpose*—we still shall always have opportunity to give, even if it only be giving by our presence encouragement to the newcomers and others. Remember your first meeting? Wouldn't you have had an awful shock if there *no one* else had been there? And it could happen, if all went to meetings for only what the meeting had to offer. But on the other hand, there would always be a huge crowd if all went for what they could give—for there then could never be a reason or even an excuse for staying away.

"Were *all* made sober? Where then are the other nine?"

"So that you, being sobered, may in turn sober others."

"For it is in *giving* that we receive…"

That's right—this is a *give* program. Remember?

What else besides our presence at the meetings can we *give?*

Let's analyze a few more.

2. **We can give of our knowledge and experience** to the discussion during the meeting. We can give our own perspective and bury all destructive habits of criticizing the talk, or the speaker, or the other members, or what goes on in the group. We can *give* encouragement to the speaker, ever mindful of how we expect a handshake, a thank you or a pat on the back after we have spoken or led a meeting. "For it is in *giving* that we receive..."

   Once there was a very famous public speaker whom all seemed to applaud and compliment after every speech. One day an elderly woman said to the speaker after one of his fine talks, "You must, sir, get a lot of satisfaction out of all the compliments that are paid you after every talk you give."

   "Not at all," he replied. "You see, madam, all of that just runs off like water off a duck's back."

   "That I know, sir," she insisted with a twinkle in her eye, "but sure the duck likes it!"

3. **We can give our attention to the talk.** This is really the only way we can ever hope to receive much from even the best of talks. They who jabber on and on with their neighbor while the speaker holds forth; they who take a little nap during the talk; they who are thinking about the thousand and one things of the day instead of listening *attentively* to what is being said—all of these can *take* little home with them for they *fail* to give the first requisite: *attention*. "Where are the other nine?" Some, I believe, are sleeping!

4. **We can give an open mind** to the meeting and the talk and the discussion. The Big Book tells us: "Willingness, honesty, and open-mindedness are essentials of recovery. But they are indispensable." It is the closed mind that begets criticisms, and doubts, and monotonies, and boredom, and dislikes and all the other things that eventually make for *missing* meetings. We *must* give to every talk or discussion an *open mind*. It is essential. "So

that we being strengthened in our society may in turn strengthen our fellowman."

5. **We can give our own self-reflection** to the talk or discussion—not the other fellow's. How often do we hear the remark, "Boy, I hope Jim was listening tonight. He really *needed* that talk." We shall never get much from the talk to improve our sobriety and our living unless we apply what is said to ourselves—not to the person sitting in the next row. And it is only when we apply what is said to our lives that we can take it home with us. "If the shoe fits, wear it." Then it will still be there when you get home. But it won't be there if you put it on someone else's foot!

6. **We can give action on what we hear.** To merely listen and then proceed to forget what was said will never bear fruit in our lives. It is only *action* on what we hear that will do that.

The story is told of a certain fellow who was consistently late for services on Sunday at his church. In those days the sermon was always given *after* the services. So this Sunday morning, he was hurrying to church and as he approached the steps he noticed the people beginning to leave. He accosted a woman who came down the steps and queried why so many were leaving church. And he asked, "Is the sermon over?"

"No, it is not," was her short reply.

"Then why are so many leaving church, madam, if the sermon isn't over?"

"Because the priest has stopped speaking," she again answered tersely.

"Come now. You say that the sermon is not over. And now you say that the priest has stopped speaking. What do you mean?"

"Indeed, sir, the priest *has* stopped speaking. But the sermon now only *begins*. For we take it home to continue it and use it in our daily lives!"

We learn in order to use—so that we "may in turn strengthen ourselves and our fellowman." *Action is the magic word!*

7. **We can give encouragement** to the newcomers and to those having difficulties with their living or the program. In short, we can give a good shoulder to them to cry on. Remember when you needed just such a shoulder? Be a good listener. *Give* an ear. Don't join the "other nine" who always sidestep the newcomers and the problem folks. Want to keep your courage? Then give a little!

8. **We can give a talk once in a while** when asked. And no matter how poorly trained you may be in speaking, you can give a talk, and a good one. Remember you are only there as the instrument anyway. What are you going to say? Well, that's in the Big Book too: "Tell them what happened to *you*." That is really all that you have to give. And that is what everyone wants to hear: what has happened to you in A.A., how the program is working in your daily living. You say it isn't? Well, then tell them just that—for that is what happened to you. And always bear in mind, *Someone somewhere is waiting for that very particular thing in your talk which is in no one else's and which is the very thing that is going to give them or strengthen their sobriety.* "That you being strengthened, you may in turn strengthen your fellowman." Give of *yourself* therefore in your talk in all honesty and simplicity. Such talks don't have to be practiced—they are always *inside*.

9. **We can give our time and talent for service:** to chair the meeting, the picnic, or the annual banquet; to take on the job of secretary. This is all practicing the Twelfth Step. This is all *giving*. But here in particular there is much "avoiding." Perhaps it is because in these jobs and similar ones in the group activities, one has to *give* a lot: of time, of thought, of talent, and particularly of *patience* in weathering the barbs of the "aginers," and the "slingshot artists." But let us never forget, the *more* we give, the *more* we receive—from *God*—not from the others in the group. With this in mind, one will do such a job in the

group and not tend to be discouraged and disappointed when the wolves come a-running. For whatever happens, we *always* then *accomplish* what we set out to do—to *give*. "This is a *give* program."

10. **We can give the Big Book** to those we sponsor or to those who haven't the financial means to buy one. The neglect of doing this is in the writer's opinion one of the biggest canchre sores of A.A. today. It is amazing how many, many so-called members of A.A. don't own the Big Book, nor have they ever even read it. Why is this? In most cases because their sponsor was too "tight" in his sobriety to buy them the book. It's all in the book. That's the therapy of A.A. from the ones who started this thing. It tells "how it works" as it was meant to work—effectively proven from experience.

To give some idea of how widespread this lack of the Big Book is, consider this true story. A member of A.A. from the southern California coast, where every meeting might include part of the Big Book's fifth chapter read aloud, was traveling elsewhere in the country and dropped in on an A.A. meeting in a strange town. Learning that he was from a distant group, the chairman ask him to speak. He said, "Sure, get me the Big Book."

"Big Book?" queried the chairman in confusion, "What is the Big Book?"

Their group—the whole group—had never heard of the Big Book! I would have loved to hear the gentleman-from-California's talk that evening!

Distributing and *giving* the Big Book and other A.A. literature to other alcoholics is "carrying the message" and all part of the Twelfth Step work. Whereas knocking or libeling or minimizing the Big Book and other A.A. literature is not carrying the message but *stymieing* that message.

11. **We can give of our money** to help the group help others who suffer. And here is the enigma of A.A.: How "tight" an

alcoholic may become after being sober in A.A.! And I also know that too many A.A.'s just don't give. Ingratitude? Is it thoughtlessness? I don't know why. But I *do* know it.

Many groups are plagued by this "enigma." One of the prime sources of trouble in A.A. is financial. And let the secretary, chairperson, or anyone else ask for a bit of "extra" money for this or that, and the howl of protest sometimes reaches to the highest heavens. And although tattered and torn, that now aged excuse struts through each echo: "No dues, no fees—A.A. don't cost nuthin'." "You can't buy sobriety." And "We have nothing to sell."

Very true. We have nothing to sell. We cannot buy sobriety. There are no dues nor fees in A.A. *But* we have an awful lot to give away. And not the least of the things we have is some of that green stuff that wasn't there when we were drinking. That too was given to us to share it in turn with our fellow man.

You say you *worked* for what you have? Maybe you did, bub, but *who gave you* the ability, and the talent, and the health, and the job that brought what you have? *Better* give some back else that same One Who gave it to you may some day take it all away again. It *has* happened on one grand and glorious binge! What is that we have been repeating? "We keep *only what we give away;* for it is in giving that we receive." Now how about that extra buck or so for the kitty or for the General Headquarters or just for the sake of giving! This is a *"give"* program. Let it not be said in your group when the kitty is counted, "What? Only *one* buck? Where are the other nine?"

12. **Finally, we can give of the special talents** with which God may have endowed us and by the use of those talents "strengthen our fellow man."

To many individuals God has given special talents. They are given so that these individuals in turn may use them to also "carry the message" to alcoholics. If you have talent to write, carry the message that way. To some, other talents are given. Those too we can give; talents of entertaining, of speaking, of teaching. When we use these talents in A.A. to help our fellow members, no matter what type of help that might be, we are *giving* of ourselves. And so in that giving we shall again receive—more help, more sobriety, more serenity, more of everything that is good and desirable. For all talents are given; they are gifts of God, and we give them back when we use them for our fellow people.

Undoubtedly many of our readers have heard the famed story of the juggler. It is told on radio and television and by word of mouth each Christmas time. But it is so striking and has some bearing on this use of talent that we give it now for your thoughtful analysis.

There once lived a juggler. He was very expert at juggling, but he was also very poor. One Christmas Eve, he visited the monastery church to pray. And as he knelt there in the shadows, he saw the monks entering the chancel and in single file wend their way to the statue of the Virgin. As each one reached the statue, he paused and in humble reverence placed something at her feet. Curious, the juggler inched toward one of the monks who had been to the statue and then return to one of the pews to kneel in prayer. He nudged the monk.

"Father," he whispered, "what is it that all of you were doing tonight going to the statue of the Virgin?"

"We were all placing at her feet our Christmas gift—something each had made himself during the year. It is our token of gratitude to our Lady on Christmas."

The juggler returned to his place in the shadows with a heavy heart. He had nothing to give the Lady for Christmas. And he was so poor he could buy nothing. And he knew no art nor trade, so he could make nothing for her. Then suddenly a thought came to his wondering mind. "The only thing I have is my juggling. I shall juggle for the statue. That, small as it is, will be my Christmas present."

He approached the statue, and in full view of the monks, he juggled. They were horrified at this apparent sacrilege. They rushed to the altar and were about to stop him when suddenly they all saw a strange, yes, a miraculous sight. The Lady waving them back—and in Her eyes there shone a light of heavenly joy, and across Her lips there played a beautiful smile, a smile of approval to the poor juggler.

He *gave* what he had. And thus he received the approval of heaven.

"For it is in giving that we receive," and A.A. is a *give* program.

What to give? That is simple. We only have to paraphrase the Big Book's suggestion that we tell others our own experience: "Give whatever was given to you!"

One of the most heartwarming experiences the writer has had recently was to see the many A.A.'s in Hollywood groups so frequently *giving* of their talents to entertain, to encourage, to help along someone or some special A.A. effort. Time and time again those in the entertainment industry were *giving what was given to them*. No wonder A.A. enjoys such phenomenal growth in those parts. What is it that we hear so often? "It is God who giveth the increase."

Gratitude and Sponsorship

"What we give away—we keep."

Our biggest opportunity to give in A.A. is in calling upon and sponsoring some alcoholic who still has not known of the blessing of sobriety through Alcoholics Anonymous. In doing so we fill two people's needs—theirs and ours. And it is only when we get that conviction—once and for all—that we shall sincerely accept sponsorship in A.A. And it is only in *keeping* that conviction that we shall *continue* to sponsor others and to mature in sobriety and serenity. Because "it is only in giving that we receive; and what we give away—we keep."

The drinking alcoholic, the alcoholic who, still in his confusion and sickness, is looking for the door that will lead him out of his darkness and despair to the light of true sobriety, needs you. But never forget, chum, you need him just as desperately if you want to permanently and contentedly keep that sobriety that you now enjoy and which some other alcoholic gave to you. Again we repeat as we stressed in the early pages, that is the only way you will keep your sobriety. And if you have a doubt, just ask the next "slippee" you meet, especially if he happens to be one who was sober for a "long while in A.A." before he slipped.

Let's write it in our minds and hearts with never-to-be-erased letters: *Giving in A.A. is self-preservation.* This is a *selfish* program; and so it must be a give program. "What we give away—we *keep.*"

And the most essential *giving* in A.A. is in making Twelfth-Step calls and sponsorship. In no other activity of the Twelfth Step do we give so much of ourselves as we do in sponsoring the new member, in making a Twelfth-Step call. Time, talent, money, sobriety, encouragement, guidance—we give our all. And yet, isn't it true that in most groups only a minority are willing to make Twelfth-Step calls, only a few are willing to sponsor other alcoholics? "Were not *ten* made sober? Where then are the other nine?" You know where they are? They are basking at present in the sunshine of their own sobriety. And it won't be too long—maybe a year, or two or three, or even eight or ten—but sooner or later, and soon at the latest, that sobriety which they are now so closely keeping to themselves, is going to become awfully boring, and heavy, and a terrible burden. And to such a "stinking," stingy, self-centered mentality, there will be only one apparent easement—the bottle. Again, we suggest: ask the next "slippee" you meet. He found out—the hard way.

Ingratitude? Thoughtlessness? Laziness? I know not, but I do know it is true. So how about you and me? Let's keep what we have.

Let's improve our sobriety, our serenity, our whole theme of living. Let's *give* in sponsorship. For even though we don't want to, or even if we don't like to, or even if we feel it's a burden; the truth from experience tells us over and over again: *We got to!* "Selfish gratitude"—the A.A. paradox.

Practical Sponsorship

"This is a give program."

A sincere A.A. may make many mistakes in his Twelfth-Step calls and in sponsoring new members, but on the average he *won't be hurt thereby,* nor will he seriously hurt his protégé. For the sincere person is more than any other an instrument in the hands of the Almighty, and *He* will give or permit whatever results. And after all, as we pointed out previously, the sincere person making a Twelfth-Step call or sponsoring a new member has accomplished his purpose no matter how blundering or erroneous may have been his "technique" for he has *given,* and in the giving has kept and improved his own sobriety.

But years of A.A. experience have yielded some lessons as to what works best and what is best left undone. There are no "dues nor fees" in A.A. And likewise, no matter what experience might point out, there are also no "do's nor don'ts." Each member's autonomy forms the basic solidarity of the entire A.A. membership. So all members do their A.A. in the way *they choose to do it.* Nor is there ever to be anyone to bid him or her or them "nay." However, common sense demands that we *for our own* sakes ordinarily follow the paths which experience demonstrates to the better. So the following guides (we hesitate to label them "rules") are merely given as a result of our own experience and the experiences of thousands in A.A., which we have picked up here and there. So for succinctness and using our literary license, we shall here and there use "do" and "don't" or maybe even to "be sure to", *but* when we do, just remember you *don't* gotta!

First let's answer a few questions, from the author's personal viewpoint.

How many should one person sponsor at one time?

The answer to this question must always be relative. Such a number will always vary greatly between those who work twelve hours a day and those with no job or family obligation. But there are ways and means of judging how many one can prudently sponsor at one time. We can sponsor *only that number to whom we can give the full benefit of our sponsorship.* Many get into difficulty here, and neglect is the result simply because in their eagerness they make many calls, but have not the time to give these same new "babies" the attention that true sponsorship demands. It is certainly much better to sponsor *one* and *give* him or her the *full* benefit of our time, than it is to sponsor *many* and then neglect the follow-up in the "other nine." We feel that an average sincere A.A. will be always sponsoring *one* new member, although at times because of lack of prospects or of time difficulties, such will go for a time without a prospect "under his wing." Whether you can sponsor more than one at the same time, will depend entirely on how much time you have to give. May we suggest: give what you have, to whomsoever asks, whenever time permits.

How soon should a new member sponsor somebody else?

In handling this question, we find all sorts of "rules," "regulations," and "traditions" in various groups and areas. And as with so many things in A.A., there exists a wide difference of opinion, varying from "not for at least a year" to "the sooner the better." In between we find the six-month rule, the ninety-day rule, the six-month continued sobriety rule and what have you. Let us analyze the reasons they adduce and then let's try to evaluate the one which seems to "follow the program."

Those groups and individuals who maintain that a member must be "dry" for six months or a year before sponsoring a new member, or making a Twelfth-Step call, give the following reason: "You do not level off in A.A. for six months or a year; you can't learn A.A. in a few days or weeks; so you can't tell the newcomer much about A.A. until you have been a member for a sufficient length of time."

In our opinion, this reasoning places too much emphasis on "learning" and "teaching," whereas we feel that such really are unimportant in A.A. After all, the Big Book tells us, "Tell them what happened to you." And certainly everyone is quite conscious of what happens from their first day of sobriety—in fact *more* conscious of it immediately than six months or a year later.

So we think that the best procedure is to sponsor someone—the sooner the better. (Of course we are presuming that the one who starts sponsoring is *completely* sober and not still reeking!)

A.A is not a *learn* program; it is not a *teach* program; it is a give program. Remember?

And what has a person who has been sober only a week to give? A week of sobriety! Which is a week more than the one on whom he is calling has. And such a one, with only a week of sobriety, certainly has the qualifications asked for in the Big Book—and which are so simple: *"Tell them what happened to you;"* and which interpreted means: *"Give!"* Surely length of sobriety does not determine one's ability to do that.

How much attention should one give in sponsoring?

Perhaps the biggest *"do"* we should quote here is *"Do avoid using excuses."* And we might add that it is difficult to *give* too much. However, there is often present the danger of "spoiling" or "over-pampering" the new prospect. We don't want to unwittingly echo any of the enabling that may have contributed to the person's past drinking. And in our experience we feel there are more "slips" occasioned (We hesitate to use the word "caused") by too much pampering than by too much neglect. The sincere sponsor will endeavor to avoid both extremes. But it is impossible to determine what is too much and what is too little in general. Every alcoholic, although having the same basic problem and pattern, has a *different need*. How can we determine that? There is only one sure method: *Stop. Ask for the right answer in humble prayer, and then act.* The results then are truly in the hands of God—where they should be.

How often should one call again on a "slippee"?

We shall answer this by giving the reply once given by a member of one of the Midwestern groups during an A.A. Forum.

In this group was a fellow who again and again slipped. Seventeen times he slipped; and seventeen times one of the members of the group answered his call for help. And then the group all decided to call a halt and agreed that the next time no one would go to see him if he slipped.

A few weeks passed, and once again the unfortunate fellow slipped. Frantically again he called the group for help. All refused—save *one*. One member decided to make the call. The "slippee" sobered up again—and to this day never has had another drink and is a solid member of the group!

Their curiosity having been aroused after this one member had made the call, the rest of the group asked him why he had made it, particularly after all had agreed not to. His answer is a classic: "When he called for help, I got to figuring and decided that if I *didn't* go, I was *sure* to lose all the effort expended on the other seventeen calls. So I went."

So, how often? Your guess is as good as mine. We just can't presuppose on the Lord. We can only *give*.

Practical guidelines for sponsors

And now a few "guides" for what they may be worth. We did not pick them out of books. They are only our conclusions as a result of experience. They are not rules, not even suggestions, but only what in our humble opinion have worked in many, many instances.

1. *Always follow up every call.* Don't be a "one-call-that's-all" fellow or gal. If we make a Twelfth-Step call, let's follow through on it. Let's see that the one we have called on gets to a meeting, etc., etc. And even if it is one of those "not-yet-ready" individuals, it is a good idea to "look-in" every once in a while. We can never know just when he might be ready.

2. *Do not be alarmed at initial zeal.* So many new members go all out in the beginning and try to sober up every person they can find—in the jails, hospitals, skid-row, etc. Let them go! They aren't doing any harm. They may not have much success, as we all know, but it is all a part of such a personality's maturing. So let us not criticize, not forbid them, nor become alarmed. Let them make all the calls, cold or otherwise, they want to.

3. *Don't expect success.* And don't fear failure. Let us remember what we said earlier about "motive." We make Twelfth-Step calls in order to give what we have so that in giving what we have we shall be enabled to keep what we have. We are not

making the calls to *sober up the other fellow, nor to keep the other fellow sober by sponsoring him.* We make the call; we sponsor a new prospect *only* to *keep* what *we have.* Selfish gratitude! Such a motive will keep down pride; it will prevent many heartaches and disappointments.

4. *Don't brag.* We ought not to brag to the new fellow about *our own sobriety,* nor should we brag about the *wonderful* fellows and gals in the group. Nor should we indicate that there are many "big shots" socially, or otherwise in the group, even if we do not use their names. We *do not have anything to SELL.* All we have is *ourselves* to *GIVE* away—by *"telling them what happened to you!"*

5. *Exclude no one.* If one is *honest* and *humble* and *sincere,* he will make a Twelfth-Step call and sponsor *all who* ask—whether they be black or white; rich or poor; Catholic, Protestant, or Jewish; coming off a drunk or completely sober.

   We also feel that it is foolish concern, irrelevant, and ineffective to endeavor to have someone of "equal" social status or profession to make the call. The effectiveness of the A.A. approach lies in one alcoholic talking to another alcoholic, not in a lawyer talking to a lawyer, not a doctor talking to a doctor, nor a clergyman talking to a clergyman, nor a laborer talking to a laborer.

6. *Let medical needs be judged by someone capable of judging.* Dispense no medicine to the alcoholic, whether drunk or sober. Only a qualified professional may safely do this. On the average, whenever a prospect seems to us to be very sick or very drunk, we still are not capable of judging whether hospitalization is needed. When there is doubt, *let doctors make that decision.* That is their profession, not ours. And by incompetently deciding *not* to hospitalize a sick alcoholic, we may do a lot of harm or even occasion death.

7. *Always see to it that the prospect gets a copy of the Big Book.* In our opinion this *"do"* is the most important of them all and could profitably be placed in large lettering in all A.A. club rooms and meeting halls. Always give the prospect a Big Book!

8. *Don't practice what you are going to say to the prospect.* Rehearsing what we are going to say leads to "selling" the

program. And we don't have anything to sell through a sales talk. "Tell them what happened to you." We all know that *very* well. And we do not need *practice to relate it*. But you know something? We might need a little *humility!*

The founder of A.A. in Indianapolis was asked in a meeting one time what he thought about on the way to call on a new fellow. He answered in his own simple yet sincere way: "I don't think about anything. *I pray.*"

We think he has something there!

9. *Don't give professional advice.* Many times harm is done and the new member is left more confused than ever simply because his sponsor assumed the professional role of doctor or psychiatrist. Medical advice should be given only by doctors; psychiatric advice should be given only by competent psychiatrists. Tread carefully with religious matters, too; clergy and spiritual care professionals are best equipped for this. Whenever our "sponsee" asks for such advice, guide him or her to one who is competent by profession to give it, and don't in egotistical vanity give it yourself. Remember, chum, it is the fellow's body, mind, or soul you're dealing with, and that ain't unimportant.

The same thing holds true relative to serious family problems. On the average, we are not competent, nor should we ever presume to advise in such problems. Guide the new member to one who is competent to do so. Rash advice given by A.A.'s on family problems and relationships has often done untold harm and damage. And on occasion such presumptuous dribble has broken up a family where it was not necessary.

The only thing we can give advice about is *drinking—* and there is an awful lot about that we still don't know.

10. *If possible, take someone along on calls.* There are several very sound reasons for this. In the first place, it is prudent security. For we can never know what circumstances we are going to run into on a call. And many, many times having someone along is self-protection—morally, physically, and legally.

Moreover, it will often prove more effective in making contact. If one of us happens to irritate the new prospect, the other may seem more worthy of confidence.

11. *Don't give money on calls.* Giving money to the individual on whom we are calling is always bad practice. Our own charity shall dictate whom to help and whom not to help financially, but it should not be part of a Twelfth-Step call. If there is definite need, and we feel inclined to fill that need, then give it to a third party to use for the prospect. A.A. does not deal with financial problems; nor does the program offer guidance about giving, lending, or paying anyone else in A.A. What one does in this matter of money is up to each one to decide. As in politics and religion, so also in money affairs: each member does what he or she chooses to do and in the way one chooses. Although we may remark that in most instances financial transactions between A.A.s or in A.A. end up in much difficulty and misunderstanding. That is why we are advised in the Big Book to keep *politics, religion, and finance out of A.A.* So whatever one does in these matters ought to be transacted outside and away from meetings and other A.A. settings.

12. *Avoid sponsoring someone with whom a romantic relationship could develop.* This longstanding guideline, it is felt, helps prevent the "Thirteenth-Step" development of romantic relationships that can complicate recovery.

13. *Don't preach or moralize to the prospect.* We are not calling on the alcoholic for the purpose of saving a soul. We are making the call to *give* what we *have* so we shall be enabled to *keep* what we *have*. And that is *sobriety*. He or she will get a lot more—*later—and in his or her own way.* Give him God, but don't try to impose *your* beliefs upon him. Let's keep in mind: most alcoholics *have been subjected to preachments and moralizing thousands of times,* and by experts—but *it did not take.* So let's simply get the person sober first—physically and mentally. Then let us *let God* do the rest.

14. *Don't avoid or apologize for God.* On the other hand, let's not be the person who, for fear of "scaring" the prospect, won't even bring up the subject of God. Prudent "giving" of God never cured anyone, *but not even mentioning God has often*

left the newcomer with no support to turn to, and a slip may then be more likely. Go read your Big Book. It has an excellent treatise on how to broach God to the person on a call. *It's all in the book.*

15. *Don't look down on the prospect.* We should never be patronizing in our approach. We are not helping a poor drunk— *we are making the calls to help us.* What did we say about motives? We certainly can and should feel genuine sorrow for the plight of the individual in the throes of coming out of a glorious binge. We can pity. We can sympathize. But our purpose of being there should never be patronizing—with the idea of helping the "poor devil" out. Let us not forget that we need him or her as much, if not quite so urgently, as that person needs us. We are giving in order to keep what has been given to us. Selfish gratitude—the A.A. paradox!

16. *Don't force sobriety.* It just cannot be done—permanently. We may force one to stop drinking as of here and now by forcefully taking him or her away from all liquor. But unless he or she wants to stop now, it is foolish and a waste of time and never effective to *make* that person stop now.

    On many occasions, in order to save his or her job, an individual has been forced to sober up. *But that binge will happen sooner or later.* And for the good of all concerned, it is much better to let the person finish it here and now than to have it continue from where you interrupted it later on and with only added heartaches and problems.

    If the one upon whom we call is not ready to quit, *let him or her continue* and remind the person: "Call us when you are ready."

17. *Don't gossip about or reveal what happens on a call.* In making Twelfth-Step calls it often happens that we are let in on many family and personal problems and secrets. *Let them die within yourself.* It really is a damnable thing to hear someone bragging and gossiping about what he found, or saw, or heard on a Twelfth-Step call. Gossip itself is a detestable habit, but when it has to do with what we learn in confidence, it becomes truly diabolical. Tell the person you are calling on what happened to *you*, but do not tell others what happened on a Twelfth-Step call.

18. *Don't make promises.* It is both presumptuous and a false premise to promise to the new prospect what the future will bring if he or she joins A.A. So many do this only to pave the way for later disappointments, self-pity, and the eventual slip. We cannot guarantee that the new member, by joining A.A., will get a job back or family back or make a lot of money or anything else materially. The only thing we know is that if he or she follows the program sincerely the person will stay sober and *can* be happy. What else may happen is entirely in the hands of the Almighty. And hard facts point to the truth that most A.A.'s have as many or more problems, hardships, and difficulties *after* they are on the program. But if they are on the program they retain both sobriety and serenity *in spite of* problems and hardships and difficulties. A.A. will give peace of mind, serenity, happiness, and sobriety, but not necessarily a better job, more money, more pleasure, or even better health. (In case you do not realize it, there is a big difference between happiness and pleasure. In fact, people who have most pleasures are usually the least happy.)

   Such false promises are often made from the speaker's podium in A.A. meetings as well as on Twelfth-Step calls. We have many times listened in silent musings and amusement while the speaker painted a glowing, though false, picture of the endless material benefits that would inevitably accrue to every member of A.A.—a bigger and better job; more income; a better home; better health; and endless pleasures. The speaker left out the bottle pleasures—but will come to that, we fear—in a month or two or more!

19. *Be sure the prospect and his or her family know how to get in touch with you.* If you hesitate to do this for fear of being unduly disturbed, then it is better not to make the call at all. It is, in the writer's opinion, ridiculous to only tell the person that you are "Bill from A.A or Kathy from A.A." In this way, you will still be a non-entity. And how in the world a member of A.A. can tell the new person much about him- or herself, and not reveal one's full name, is difficult to understand. The tradition of anonymity respects the public level and the media. And yet there are a few groups who advise members *never* to tell one's last name—not even to the other members

of the group. No wonder they enjoy snail-like growth. "Tell the person what happened to you," but *tell him or her who you are.*

20. *Do—or don't—make cold calls, as you choose.* There always has been and still is much discussion on whether to call on a person with the idea of giving sobriety, even though such a person has not asked anyone to call. These are the so-called "cold calls." And we feel it is entirely up to an individual whether he or she wants to make such. And certainly neither the one who makes such calls nor the one who refuses to make them are to be condemned. In fact, no one in A.A., no matter how he or she works the program, is to be condemned. That too is God's business.

21. *Don't prognosticate.* It is the height of folly to prophesy who will and who will not "make the program." The longer we are in A.A., the more we realize how impossible it is to pin the label of success or failure on a newcomer. We all tend to do this at least within ourselves, until after a time we find we have been 99.9 percent wrong; and then we take the sensible attitude. *Anyone* may make it, and *anyone* may not make it. There is again only one prognostication we can with certitude give the newcomer: "If you follow the A.A. program sincerely, you will make it no matter who you are, what your background is, what your problems are, or whatever else may or may not be present in the circumstances of your living. All that is needed is willingness—nothing else."

22. *Don't tell a new member whether he or she is alcoholic or not.* Much damage and many slips have resulted in some wiseacre's judging that so-and-so is not an alcoholic. The person's age is not a factor; even in the teens one can already be an alcoholic. To quote from the Big Book, "If one says he is an alcoholic he is ready for A.A." The *only* one to make the judgment of readiness for A.A. therefore is *the individual.*

23. *Don't "over-Twelfth-Step."* Although we can fundamentally never give too much, circumstances can make it so that our giving becomes excessive. So in Twelfth-Step activity, in making calls, in sponsoring new members, we can *overdo* it by taking ourselves away from our family too often or by overtiring ourselves.

An axiom of Alcoholics Anonymous is "A.A. comes first." But that does not mean A.A. *activities.* It means that the *principles we have learned in A.A.* come first. And one of the first principles we learn is: "First things first." And the order of prudent charity tells us that *we come first.* For we are told to "love our neighbor *as ourselves,*" which means we must love ourselves *first.* So if our Twelfth-Step activities such as sponsorship and making calls are *injurious to* us, then it is time to eliminate some of those activities. And if it is overtiring us, we are definitely being hurt, and badly. Many an otherwise good, sincere A.A. has learned the hard way—by a slip—that as alcoholics we cannot tolerate becoming overtired for a prolonged period. If we do, we are in danger of setting off that craving for drink over which we will have no control.

We also learn from true charity that our families come next. So if our Twelfth-Stepping is hurting our home relationship and causing us to neglect our family, we should eliminate some of the Twelfth-Step activities.

24. *Don't hesitate to use any reasonable adjunct to aid in helping the new person stay sober.* In many groups there are traditions of procedure wherein varied psychological helps are employed in Twelfth-Step activity to give an added boost to those in early recovery.

    The use of "tokens," we feel, is very effective and the experience of many groups has borne this out. Now called medallions or coins—originally poker chips, in the early days of A.A.—these tokens symbolize the holder's length of time in sobriety. While originally intended to help those in earliest recovery, they now serve as an ongoing reminder of our daily reprieve as recovering alcoholics.

    Sometimes the new prospect who wants to stay sober is given a chip on the first contact, and the caller tells him or her that the chip is merely a *token* of sobriety. The caller may suggest that if the prospect should ever be tempted to take that first drink, the token could be a reminder to pray first, to call a sponsor or other sobriety supporter, or perhaps even to toss the token aside before taking the drink. We have had some very dramatic happenings as the result of this token-therapy, and some are truly amazing. For example:

John Doe was given a white poker chip by his sponsor when he made the call on John. He explained its purpose. Some weeks later, on a business trip, everything went wrong for John and in his resentment he decided to get a drink. He took his car keys from his pocket to start the car and lo, the token came with them. He looked at it, hesitated, then mused: "Well, I'll drive over to the next town before I get the drink." He came to the next town, drove up to the tavern and went in. He reached into his pocket for some change. Out came the token. His conflict heightened. He veritably crushed the chip in his clenched hand. Then the thought: "God—ask for help." That's what his sponsor had said. And as John so proudly relates his story, "For the first time in my life I said a humble sincere prayer. And I left the tavern relaxed and relieved and to this day, nine years later, I still haven't taken that first drink." This actually happened!

25. *Don't neglect the alcoholic's physical needs.* This fact in sponsorship is many times sadly neglected. Much can be done to smooth the rugged first weeks or months of the newcomer by pointing out to him or her and stressing the fact that the body has a lot to do with the alcoholic sickness, and that the average body needs a lot of nutritive reconditioning and readjustment before normalcy sets in. And a competent physician, one who is thoroughly acquainted with alcoholism and its particular needs, can help the body to "level off" and readjust. Such a doctor can and will also point out body needs that will prove very helpful to the alcoholic for the rest of his or her sober life. Doctors tell us that the average alcoholic's physical processes will have specific and added needs for all of the years of sobriety.

So even though your prospect does not need hospitalization, practically every alcoholic can with great profit consult a competent physician after quitting drinking, and it is the course of wise sponsorship to guide your newcomer to a doctor—one who is familiar with alcoholics and alcoholism.

And as the Twelfth Step says, in all of our calls and our sponsoring, and in "all of our affairs, we *practice* these principles." And practice means repeat day in and day out, hour in and hour out, and, if necessary, minute in and minute out. "Practice makes perfect" is an old axiom. And in A.A. it is the secret of success and of serenity. A great artist in the musical world sometimes reverts to mediocrity, even to oblivion. Why? The musician stopped practicing. The person kept on playing, that is, applying musical knowledge and skills, but without practice he or she soon lost both knowledge and skills.

So too with many A.A.s—they learned "these principles," but they sooner or later ceased practicing them. And then they lost both principles and sobriety. Ask any long-time slippee. "Practice these principles in *all* of our affairs" means that we must *continue to give* in *all* of our living. And giving of all these principles may be summed up in one final sentence, one final *give,* one final "should"—we should give an *example of total sobriety* in all that we do!

- in business
- in our spiritual life
- in our home life
- in social life
- in our A.A. group life

Total sobriety—that means happy sobriety; calm sobriety; virtuous sobriety; honest sobriety; loving sobriety; willing sobriety; open-minded sobriety; always using *all* of the principles we have learned in A.A. in *all* of our affairs. We must be ready and willing to share and to give all that we have to whomsoever asks when they ask.

Take a quick look around A.A. We see thousands who are not only sober, but happy; they are *totally* sober. Would you like to join their ranks? Then give—give—give; again we say *give.* Or else you will remain with "the other nine"—possibly sober, but not happy; possibly still an A.A., but missing many meetings; possibly still "dry," but gradually, oh so gradually "slipping"; yes, possibly *drunk*—for this is above all else a *give* program.

And need we remind you that you are sober today only so that "you, being sobered, may in turn sober your fellow person"? And need we stress again the paradox which is the essence of A.A. and should motivate every member in his or her "giving:" *In the process of sobering your fellow person, you in turn will be strengthened in your own sobriety? Selfish gratitude!*

For "what we give away—we keep; for it is in the giving that we receive . . . and when we die, we take with us only that which we have given away."

There ain't no choice!

Imprimatur.
✠ PAUL C. SCHULTE
Archbishop of Indianapolis

THE TWELVE STEPS

1. We admitted we were powerless over alcohol—that our lives had become unmanageable.

2. Came to believe that a Power greater than ourselves could restore us to sanity.

3. Made a decision to turn our will and our lives over to the care of God *as we understood Him.*

4. Made a searching and fearless moral inventory of ourselves.

5. Admitted to God, to ourselves, and to another human being the exact nature of our wrongs.

6. Were entirely ready to have God remove all these defects of character.

7. Humbly asked Him to remove our shortcomings.

8. Made a list of all persons we had harmed, and became willing to make amends to them all.

9. Made direct amends to such people wherever possible, except when to do so would injure them or others.

10. Continued to take personal inventory and when we were wrong promptly admitted it.

11. Sought through prayer and meditation to improve our conscious contact with God *as we understood Him,* praying only for knowledge of His will for us and the power to carry that out.

12. Having had a spiritual awakening as the result of these steps, we tried to carry this message to alcoholics, and to practice these principles in all our affairs.

The Twelve Steps are taken from *Alcoholics Anonymous,* 4th ed. (New York: Alcoholics Anonymous World Services, 2001), 59–60.

About Hazelden Publishing

As part of the Hazelden Betty Ford Foundation, Hazelden Publishing offers both cutting-edge educational resources and inspirational books. Our print and digital works help guide individuals in treatment and recovery, and their loved ones. Professionals who work to prevent and treat addiction also turn to Hazelden Publishing for evidence-based curricula, digital content solutions, and videos for use in schools, treatment programs, correctional programs, and electronic health records systems. We also offer training for implementation of our curricula.

Through published and digital works, Hazelden Publishing extends the reach of healing and hope to individuals, families, and communities affected by addiction and related issues.

For more information about Hazelden publications,
please call **800-328-9000**
or visit us online at **hazelden.org/bookstore.**